F*CK LOVE
AN ADULT COLORING BOOK
THE PERFECT ANTIDOTE TO VALENTINE'S DAY

DIANE CORMACK

I LOVE MY CAT MORE THAN YOU

COUPLED-UP DICKHEADS

love is a battlefield

He offered me a ring and I gave him the finger

I'M NOT BITTER.
I JUST FUCKING
HATE FLOWERS.

cats don't take up the whole fucking bed

CHRISTMAS IS JUST OVER FOR FUCK'S SAKE

love is a battlefield   love is a battlefield

NOTHING SAYS
I LOVE YOU BETTER
THAN A GENERIC
RING WITH
MINIMAL RESALE
VALUE

NOTHING SAYS
I LOVE YOU BETTER
THAN A GENERIC
RING WITH
MINIMAL RESALE
VALUE

He offered me a ring
and I gave him the finger

He offered me a ring
and I gave him the finger

I'M NOT BITTER.
I JUST FUCKING
HATE FLOWERS.

I'M NOT BITTER.
I JUST FUCKING
HATE FLOWERS.

you make me sick

you make me sick

LOVE is for Assholes

LOVE is for Assholes

nobody cares about your romantic evening

nobody cares about your romantic evening

CHRISTMAS IS JUST
OVER FOR FUCK'S SAKE

CHRISTMAS IS JUST
OVER FOR FUCK'S SAKE

Since when has being alone been such a damn crime?

Since when has being alone been such a damn crime?

Made in the USA
Lexington, KY
06 February 2017